Mr. Gillie Goes
to
Grammas House

Joan Mackenzie

AuthorHouse™
1663 Liberty Drive
Bloomington, IN 47403
www.authorhouse.com
Phone: 1 (800) 839-8640

Published by AuthorHouse 09/28/2018

ISBN: 978-1-5462-6151-3 (sc)
ISBN: 978-1-5462-6152-0 (e)

Print information available on the last page.

Any people depicted in stock imagery provided by Getty Images are models,
and such images are being used for illustrative purposes only.
Certain stock imagery © Getty Images.

This book is printed on acid-free paper.

authorHOUSE®

Thanks to my son Christopher for adopting Mr Gillie

Once upon a time there was a kitty called Mr Gillespie and he lived with his daddy in the big city. He loved the hustle and all the noise.

He watched the cars and people go by his house.

He also saw lots of butterflies flitting about.

He laughed and said to himself "they don't know what they are doing.

They are just flying in circles "He blinked his eyes and went to his bed and fell asleep WHAM!!

The door shuts and Mr. Gillie jumped and then
saw his Daddy and ran to him.

His daddy picks him up and says, "well Mr Gillie we have to
move so I am taking you to Grammas house to live."

So Daddy packs up all my things and my bed and puts them in the car. Well I was terrified and also excited. WE got in the car and started to drive Up hill and down dale through the country and came to a small town and stopped at a house.

"We are here!" Daddy says and there is Gramma. She picked me up and hugged me. I purred and purred .I was very happy. This was going to be fun. Gramma took me into the house and Daddy put my bed and toys down and then he said goodbye.

I was scared and ran to my bed when all of a sudden
I heard and growl and a voice said who are you
and what are you doing in my house. I opened
my eyes and here was a big orange cat the same
colour as me!! I said I am Mr Gillie and I live here.

The big orange cat said my name is Max and I live here with my sister Ruby and we don't want you here. I started crying and Gramma picked me up and told Max to be nice because I was going to be living here.

Well I settled in and went to sleep and started dreaming about butterflies. The next day I went outside and then I saw it.it was a butterfly bush. I had dreamed about it and all the butterflies around the bush. One butterfly flew near me and this beautiful voice said" hello what's your name? I said Mr Gillie what's yours? the butterfly replied that I don't have a name but I an the queen of the butterflies and welcome to our yard. I walked over to the butterfly bush and curled up in the sun and fell asleep and dreamed about the butterflies.. But that is another story...

Printed in the United States
By Bookmasters